The Malaysian Flight 370 Report

An International Search for 239 Passengers

Second Edition

JOHN WASHINGTON

CONTENTS

ACKNOWLEDGMENTS

Research Staff at CamiEyes, Inc.

1. INTRODUCTION

The Malaysia Airlines Flight MH370 has been missing for well over a week now. With each passing day, the mystery deepens as analysts, governments and global citizens at large try to decipher what happened to the ill-fated flight. It disappeared into thin air, as if by magic, without leaving a trace; reportedly, the Malaysian Air Force did not pick up any data from the missing plane as it flew across the country's airspace. Here are the ten top theories seeking to unravel this mystery:

2. DELIBERATELY DIVERTED FLIGHT

As Malaysia Airlines Flight MH370 took off from Kuala Lumpur destined to Beijing, the 227 passengers and 12 crew on board, including the two pilots, were to become the centerpiece of what has transformed into a worldwide search; unluckily though, there has been no indication of progression and families of the crew and passengers aboard the flight continue to sink deeper in desperation. In a recently formulated theory however, there is cause to believe that the missing jetliner was deliberately diverted from its set course. With what intention would anyone divert the plane? Nobody knows the answer to that yet.

Quoting from reports released by Malaysian Officials regarding the mysterious disappearance of the jetliner, whoever disabled the plane's communication system and proceeded to fly it without being detected by civilian radars must have a lot of experience and technical know-how. Aviation experts have agreed with the officials on this one given that the plane's transponder had been turned off was obviously an intentional act. Following this line of thought, Malaysian authorities led searches conducted in the homes of the pilot and his co-pilot; a formal process in their investigation. With more than 26 countries having already joined the extensive search, this theory is being relied on hoping that it will bring closure to the jetliner's disappearance. The pilot and co-pilot, being experienced in flying the jetliner, have been singled out by this theory as the prime suspects behind the disappearance of the jetliner. Investigators believe that one of the jetliner's communication systems, possibly the Aircraft and Communications Addressing and Reporting System, or ACARS, was partially disabled just as the plane flew across the east coast of Malaysia.

Although little information is known regarding the two pilots publicly, Zaharie, the 53 year old pilot, had before the mysterious disappearance posted picture of a simulator he had put together; the simulator is being scrutinized. The co-pilot, Fariq Abdul Hamid, had just recently graduated into the Boeing 777 and was reportedly contemplating marriage. Back in 2011 however, he and another pilot had invited two female passengers into the cockpit during one of their routine flights and this is a path investigators are intent on pursuing in their bid to find the truth backed by facts.

3. FIRST CYBER HIJACK

Technology has evolved with such a steady stance that some experts are proposing that the plane was cyber-hijacked in midair with the use of remote signals sent from a central device. To add to that, they also stated that the plane could also have been safely landed using the same remote controls. Though all may simply be turned away as wishful thinking, by now the advancement in technology may give life to this theory given that there are countless drones orbiting the universe; furthermore, experts have already suggested this as a possibility. With a sophisticated and advanced application, it is possible that the plane's altitude, direction and speed were all altered from a remote location and thus the disappearance of the jetliner.

According to descriptions and insights gathered from close relatives and friends, the pilot was a huge fan of gadgets since his early days and this led him to building a simulator at home. Investigators have since then taken the simulator apart with the intention of gathering any possible pointers. Anti-terror experts are also under the impression that codes created in the frameworks possessed by cyber terrorists could have advanced past the jetliner's entertainment system and taken control of the plane by overriding the security software; what's chilling is that all this could have been executed from a simple USB stick or a mobile device. The Malaysian Prime Minister, Najib Razak, revealed in a statement that the missing plane could have flown for an approximated seven hours into Kazakhstan. The executor of such a flawless plan would have to have a deep understanding of engineering system.

4. ACT OF PRIVACY

If you recall, at the onset of investigations, it had been widely suggested that two passengers who had boarded the plane using fake passports were terrorists who had taken over the plane; this theory was prematurely debunked after investigators failed to come up with evidence linking the two passengers to act of terrorism. In a new turn of events however, a US official indicated that investigators were back on this trail only that this time around, their focus was aimed at tying the jetliner's disappearance to piracy. The official went ahead to state that the plane was intentionally diverted from its original course and soon after the transponders were switched off to go stealth.

Though it is relatively improbable to fly a massive Boeing 777 under the radar for hours without raising eyebrows, it is not entirely impossible. A pilot who has spent many flight hours flying this jetliner would know exactly how to shut down all trackers, including the automated ones, with relative ease. The official was however quick to state that even for a trained terrorist, it would be a tall order to turn off all the trackers without missing a few; The jetliner's pilot had recorded an impressive 18,000 hours of flight. By landing the plane in an unspecified location and undetected, the act of piracy would have had a good chance of succeeding; only time will tell as the mystery continues to play out.

5. PILOT SABOTAGE

This particular theory has already swung the authorities into action and they intend to pursue it to its conclusion; this has been indicated by their investigations some of which have involved visiting the pilot and co-pilot's homes (both located in an up market suburb). According to new information arising from reliable sources, military radars picked up the data of an unidentified plane which is now presumed to be the ill-fated Malaysia Airlines Flight MH370. The unidentified plane was flying along a well-known navigational route; following this revelation, the search

11

for the plane was diverted from other regions to the navigational route leading towards Europe and the Middle East.

Following this commonly used navigational route, the plane might have flown towards the Bay of Bengal in the Indian Ocean. Searches have been intensified in this region though it is a pretty remote part of the ocean and has a minimal number of radar detection systems. This part of the Indian Ocean is extremely deep and finding any debris would be a lengthy process running into months if then; even then, finding the debris would be nearly impossible. This, according to the investigators, is a venture which would have been realized only with the full knowledge of the pilot. It may either have been achieved manually or by programming the auto-pilot. The attempts to shut down the transponder and the data system were done within a certain timeframe and this effectively ruled out the possibility of the plane crashing. There was a fourteen minute gap in the shutting down of these two systems, an indication that the plane had not suffered any catastrophic damage.

With the US investigation team strongly convinced that there was manual intervention, it is an indication that this could only have been actualized under the jurisdiction of a highly experienced pilot who knew just what to do in order to avoid being detected by radar.

6. EXTREME WEATHER CONDITIONS

Though this theory is not being pursued as a possible scenario given that the weather from Kuala Lumpur to Beijing was pretty calm on March 8th, it is still a viable notion given the sudden changes we experience in regard to prevailing weather conditions. In the past, poor weather has been given as the reason for the crashing of some ill-fated jetliners. Even when all seems calm, it is not uncommon to experience sudden weather conditions. In such an unprepared state, the pilots might have easily lost control of the jetliner; but then, where is the wreckage?

Back in 1985, the Delta Flight 191 took off in sunny weather from Texas only to come crushing down tragically due to a sudden microburst; this was a totally unexpected occurrence which ended 130 lives. Aboard the missing Malaysian jetliner were 239 passengers and crew whose whereabouts remain a mystery. In 1947, a flight disappeared mysteriously into the Andes Mountains; initially, investigators ruled this out as a case of pilot negligence but later, it was found out that the plane had experienced severe turbulence due to a drastic change in weather conditions. The weather pattern remained fairly stable on March 8th, the fateful day when the jetliner took off never to be seen again at this point in time.

7. REGION CONTROLLED BY THE TALIBAN

As the pilot's role in the disappearance of the plane continues to be assessed by investigators, some experts are of the belief that the missing jetliner was flying under the Pakistan radar undetected and eventually landed close to a border between Pakistan and Afghanistan. The investigators from Malaysia had earlier requested permission from the Pakistan government to follow up on this theory and see if it yields any positive results. Pakistan, however, did not pick up any data from the plane as has been suggested by the theory. In fact, the plane has never communicated with any of the Pakistan control towers.

The Pakistan authorities have cooperated with the request and promised to share any information they gather with the Malaysian investigators. Due to this theory, Pakistan is now among the 25 countries currently participating in a coordinated search for the missing jetliner. Could it have landed in Taliban territory? The last piece of communication received from the plane did not portray any distress; it was a simple "all right, good night" to the control tower. After that, communication went mum and up to date no conclusive search has come up with an idea of where the plane might be, let alone finding any far flung debris. Several satellite images had in the initial stages of investigations indicated possible locations where the plane could have crushed but eventually, they were all ruled out as they had no connection to the missing plane.

Since the Malaysian authorities have not entirely ruled out the possibility of a terror attack, it might as well be docked in the said Taliban controlled regions in Pakistan. The Kazakh Civil Aviation in Kazakhstan also reiterated that they had not detected the plane flying into their airspace; in a statement to the Malaysian investigators, the authoritative body does not downplay the possibility of the plane having flown into Kazakhstan as has been suggested by a number of theories.

8. PASSENGERS' RINGING CELL PHONE

This particular theory has led to the formulations of other theories such as one suggesting that the plane flew for hours after its disappearance. As they got desperate and anxious, friends and relatives of the passengers and crew members abroad the missing Malaysian jetliner frantically tried to reach them through their cellphones. As most of the cell phones seemed to be getting through, they ended up concluding that the plane had not crashed but for some reason, there was no response from the other end. As it is now turning out, it is possible that none of the calls made actually made it through.

When making international or long distance calls, the connection takes longer than usual as the signal tries to locate the specific cell phone number in the far away end; while doing so, it makes beeping sounds that seem to suggest the call going through. Experts have however debunked this myth stating that it is expected for such calls to display signal but not going through.

9. DEBRIS LOCATED IN CHINA

On Wednesday of the first week, China released satellite images that investigators hoped would offer the much needed insight into the disappearance of the jetliner. In the satellite images, what looked like wreckage was thought to be the missing plane and investigators didn't hesitate to validate this; it never happened though. The satellite images had picked up a gray spot in South China Sea and assessed it as possible wreckage of the ill-fated plane. Li Jiaxiang reported through the press that they had picked up smoke and floating objects in the South China Sea; at the time, they didn't confirm it as being the missing plane.

Following the release and publicizing of the satellite images, investigators from Malaysia assisted by their counterparts in Vietnam went on a frantic search in the South China Sea with the hope of finding the wreckage and finally bringing closure to this lengthy search. However, upon arriving at that part of the sea as has been suggested by coordinates in the images, the search did not yield any positive results. Whatever they found there had nothing to do with the missing Malaysian jetliner. In fact, they found literally nothing. But as far as the theory goes, the wreckage may have been washed off to that part of the sea before the investigators arrived to ascertain the truth.

Due to the huge mountain of information that continues to be churned each new day regarding the missing plane, investigators have been confused, wondering where best to focus their attention. China, being part of the 25 countries engaging in the search of the jetliner, was categorical on airing its frustrations on the gluttony of information and misinformation from every possible source. Being conducted by many countries, it is relatively hard to coordinate such a search without brushing a few shoulders. China has, as a result of their frustration announced that they might scale back on the search and take it slow as they sift through the information coming to them from the different sources.

10. PILOT SUICIDE

History has taught us not to eliminate any possibility when gathering insight into the disappearance of planes given that there has been a number of flights which crashed under the piloting of a suicidal captain. As a result of this, investigators are in the process of coming up with a conclusive answer as to whether the pilot or his co-pilot were suicidal as they steered the flight from Kuala Lumpur to Beijing. A crash caused by the pilot of the Boeing 777 category would no doubt have raised eyebrows but it didn't; maybe because the pilot chose a navigational route well known to him before crashing the jetliner.

The theory is supported by a number of expert opinions; experts state that if the plane crashed by a suicidal pilot then, there would be very little debris left to gather since the jetliner would have assumed that course with maximum speed under the control of a suicidal pilot (this explains why no wreckage of the plane has surfaced yet, eleven days into the search). Were this the case, the jetliner would then have sunk into the deep waters of Indian Ocean, a frontier which is being continually searched and monitored for the location of any debris.

If indeed the individual flying the plane at the time of its disappearance was skilled enough to evade both civilian and military radars, it is possible that the plane was safely landed, as some experts have pointed out;

something happened to this flight and nobody seems to

know why and declare it publicly.

11. FOUR WEEK UPDATE ON MH370 FLIGHT

Since March 8th 2014, the search for Malaysian flight MH370 has dragged on with no end in sight. Following this extensive search that has thus far yielded nothing, family members of the passengers continue to seek answers from the responsible authorities. There is still mild tension over how the search is being conducted with China claiming that Malaysia is withholding key information regarding the disappearance of the jetliner that had 239 people on board. Though several satellite images indicated the jetliner may have crashed into the

Southern Indian Ocean, authorities responsible for conducting the search have yet to bring it to a closure.

12. VIEWS OF AIR CHIEF MARSHAL

As the man leading the search, Air Chief Marshall Angus Houston has dampened the spirits of the passengers' relatives. Houston said that although he and his team were still searching frantically for the missing jetliner, the failure to come up with tangible results was being taken seriously. He also stated that in the event they fail to find the wreckage on the surface, he would have to, in consultation with all the parties involved in the search, strategize on what to do next; this could possibly take up to two weeks.

As the search goes on, there have been angry exchanges between Malaysian officials and Chinese relatives of those on board the jetliner. As they continue to wait for news of the plane's search effort, they have voiced concern for their missing relatives, some stating that the Malaysian officials were withholding information from them.

13. OFFICIALS AND RELATIVES' TENSION

Just after the jetliner disappeared, Malaysian officials confidently reported that the last words heard from the cockpit were "all right, goodnight". More than a fortnight later, the statement has evolved and now the officials claim that the last words were "Goodnight Malaysian three seven zero". Relatives of the passengers see this as a proof of the Malaysian officials' careless approach in relaying truthful information in a timely manner. The black box has a lifetime of one month after it is disengaged from the airplane; given that it is almost one month since the jetliner disappeared, there is little hope for its recovery. It contains vital information which would give an in-depth insight into what really happened to the jetliner.

The officials are however, quick to point out that they are stepping up efforts to find the plane's wreckage; this is contrary to speculations that the search was cooling down due to the extreme weather in the Southern part of the Indian Ocean. The region has chilly water and often experiences heavy fog. The only viable way to recover the vital black box would be by the use of sonar equipment to scan the ocean floor. To the relief of the passengers' relatives and friends, the Australian Prime Minister stated that there is no time limit as far as the search goes and that efforts will be stepped up even as the speculation levels rise by the day. With all the theories floating around, the families need assurance. In his own words, the Prime Minister categorically stated that search efforts are being increased to bring closure to the mystery of the missing plane. This is the most complicated and challenging search ever to be conducted in aviation industry.

14. PILOT'S LAST WORDS

Soon after the Malaysian transport ministry verified the transcript containing the last words, the attention has now shifted to exactly who uttered the last words; this will take time as forensic experts do not have much to work with. Even as forensics grapple with the information they have, families of the passengers aboard the plane must be wondering whether this move will bear any fruit in solving the mystery; their primary interest is for the authorities to accurately plot what happened to the plane and find any traces of the plane, assuming that it crashed. Not long after the jetliner took off, it was reportedly diverted from its course southwards; a direction in which the plane is believed to have flown for several hours before presumably crashing in the southern region of the expansive Indian Ocean.

15. AUSTRALIAN MARITIME AUTHORITY

There is no doubt whatsoever that the Australian authorities have invested heavily in trying to demystify where the plane presumably crashed. Being at the forefront, the Australian Maritime Authority has stopped giving in-depth information of any leads they find at sea; this is a sharp move as it keeps the atmosphere calm and doesn't give false hope especially to the families of the 239 passengers aboard Malaysian flight MH370. Instead, the Authority has been relaying simple statements that only cover their daily progress. The area in which the search is being conducted has remained expansive given that all previously generated leads have been invalidated after close scrutiny. At the moment, there are approximately a dozen aircraft and ten ships scouring the Indian Ocean with the hope of finding a new lead that is more promising in their quest to find the plane's wreckage in that part of the ocean. In total, about 1,100 personnel are actively involved in the search on a daily basis.

In the coming days, the highly advanced Australian naval ship Ocean Shield will be joining the search. The ship is equipped with the latest maritime technological gadgets, more notably the sophisticated US black box locator as well as an underwater drone. The ship set sail on Monday and its journey to the search area will take several days. Given that the black box battery life is designed to last thirty days even in the most hostile of environments, time is not on the ship's side. Once the black box switches off its transmission, the task to find it will be even more difficult and virtually impossible, given that they don't know where or indeed whether the plane crashed in their search region.

16. MODIFIED BOEING 737 COORDINATES

With dozens of planes hovering around the search region, coordinators of the search have acted on their worries; that of the search planes colliding in mid air due to poor visibility and the apparent lack of a suitable air control center. To counter this threat, the coordinators have settled on deploying a modified Boeing 737 to act as the air traffic controller within the region for the duration of the search. This is a crisp move on their part as they will avert disasters from happening in an already disastrous atmosphere. With the planes flying as low as 100 to 200 feet above sea level, there is an even greater chance of collision but luckily for the search team, the air traffic controller should decrease the chances of any mishaps happening. Though the air crews have high morale and hopes of finding the missing jetliner, their counterparts from the headquarters are growing weary and less confident by the day given the number of man hours that have been spent looking for leads with no positive results.

17. CONCLUSION

There are many conspiracy theories flooding social media ranging from the Bermuda Triangle to alien abduction. These theories represent sheer desperation in trying to explain what happened to the flight destined for Beijing?

Four weeks into the mystery, families and friends of the passengers and crew members aboard Malaysia Airlines Flight MH370 continue to wait patiently as the coordinated search develops new twists every day. At the moment, the only sure thing in all this is that the plane is not in the air; it either crashed and its debris can't be recovered or landed in an undisclosed location after having flown under the radar for several hours. As the mystery unravels, we will keep you posted on the latest developments as well as analyzing the most talked about theories that have been put forward.

Our prayers are with the families and friends, the passengers and crew members aboard Malaysia Airlines Flight MH370.

BOOKS NOW AVAILABLE ON
WWW.AMAZON.COM

My Hero My Traitor:
The Edward Snowden Story

The NSA:
Snowden, Obama, and the United States

Victims of Webcam Hacking 101:
What is Hacking?

Victims of Webcam Hacking 102:
Miss Teen America

Victim of Webcam Hacking 103:
Ten Ways to Avoid Webcam Hacking